The Aerialist

The Aerialist

Poems
Victoria Hallerman

For Clifford
July 12, 2016
after many gardens,
a mint iced tea
Best from a fellow poet
& blogger,
Vicki

Bright Hill Press
Treadwell, New York
2005

The Aerialist

Poems

Victoria Hallerman

2003 Winner
Bright Hill Press Poetry Award Series, No. 10
Chosen by Martin Mitchell

Cover Art and Book Design: Bertha Rogers
Editor in Chief: Bertha Rogers
Editorial Staff: Richard Bernstein, Ernest M. Fishman,
          Earl W. Roberts III, Lawrence E. Shaw
Copyright © 2005 by Victoria Hallerman - First Edition

Library of Congress Cataloging-in-Publication Data

Hallerman, Victoria.
   The aerialist : poems / Victoria Hallerman.
       p. cm. -- (Bright Hill Press poetry award series ; no. 10)
   Includes bibliographical references and index.
   ISBN 1-892471-28-0 (alk. paper)
   I. Title. II. Series: Bright Hill Press poetry book award series ; no. 10.

   PS3608.A5483A66 2005
   813'.6--dc22

                                          2005021142

The Aerialist is published by Bright Hill Press. Bright Hill Press, Inc., a not-for-profit, 501©)(3) literary and educational organization, was founded in 1992. The organization is registered with the New York State Department of State, Office of Charities Registration. Publication of *The Aerialist* is made possible, in part, with public funds from the Literature Program of the New York State Council on the Arts, a State Agency.

Editorial Address
Bright Hill Press, Inc.
94 Church Street, POB 193
Treadwell, NY 13846-0193
Voice / Fax: 607-829-5055
Web Site: www.brighthillpress.org
E-mail: wordthur@stny.rr.com

Acknowledgments

Grateful acknowledgment is made to the following journals, magazines, and anthologies for poems that originally appeared in them or will appear, sometimes in slightly different form:

AWP's *Intro 14:* "Terminal Moraine"; *Global City Review:* "Waking to Names of the Dead," "The Woman in the Magic Show"; *Grolier Prize Annual:* "When the Invisible Self Forgets"; "Discovery"/*The Nation* Program: "Moab July 1989"; *Los Angeles Review:* "The Globe" (winner of the 2003 Red Hen Poetry Award; *Lumina:* "The Sea Is a Moving House"; "Ash Grove"; *The National Poetry Competition Anthology* (Chester A. Jones Contest) : "I Know I Dream of You"; *North Dakota Quarterly:* "On the Ferry Reading Lives of the Astronomers," "The Work of the Water," "Talking to God"; *Pivot:* "Seeking Ground," "The Idea of Beauty," "Hudson River Frozen Across at Rhinecliff"; *Poetry:* "The Road Home," "We Grew Up Playing Bomb Shelter," "Sculpture by George Segal," "Doll in a Suitcase," "Egret," "A House"; *The Pushcart Prize* Anthology: "Talking to God"; *Runes:* "Children's Art, Stormlight"; *Southern Poetry Review:* "The Body Opened," "A Last Cloud."

A selection of poems appeared in each of two chapbooks, *The Woman in the Magic Show* and *The Night Market* (Firm Ground Press, 1995, 1998).

A selection of poems won the 92nd Street Y's "Discovery"/*The Nation* Prize in 1990.

Special thanks to my community in poetry, especially those who've taken time to listen and respond: Priscilla Ellsworth, Wendy Wilder Larsen, Sabra Loomis, Mary Jane Nealon, Myra Shapiro, Susan Sindall, and Janet Brof. Also, Peggy Garrison, Barbara Elovic, Laurel Blossom, Polly Howells, Nancy Kline, and Anne Vaterlaus.

Contents

Crossing in the Dark

Hearts, White, Hanging

~   ~   ~

The Woman in the Magic Show

For Dean,
who has listened since the beginning.

Crossing in the Dark

The Globe

was never accurate: as fast
as they could print the maps
it changed: Rhodesia, the Belgian Congo,
French Equatorial Africa.
       At the top of the classroom bookcase
tilted authentically on its gilded axis, it gave
a generous view of its own bottom:
Antarctica, white as a corm buried from sun.
Just above and to the right, Australia's green and gold
falling autumn leaf had a white-turned edge.

There are wrinkles in the ocean.
God's made a bad job of pasting it all down.
Mountains under the sea?
              No more a dream
than the waters that left their fossilized shells and fish
in the limestone of our sidewalks.
I drifted to school under water, clear
as the Sargasso Sea, scarlet fish
swam between my ankles, and the terrible giant squid
was a Forsythia at the corner of the schoolyard.

The river's a snake, Ohio,
in the language of the Scioto: *Beautiful River,*
         the caved-in bottom of our state.
Muddy and brown, no tides,
but if you dreamed hard it promised
to take you to the Mother of Waters,
and drifting long enough
out of the brown silted lies of the working day,
you would wake
into the blue that used to be everywhere.

Talking to God

You were in all domes,
in the Union Terminal, arching
your palm above us, who but you
could have made a sky in there and filled it up
with giants? Constellations of the WPA.
Meanwhile, every night I praised you,
squeezing my eyes shut so hard I made
meteor showers in the red and black
dome inside my head.

You lived in the Maxfield Parrish print behind
Aunt Lottie's piano,
a castle with a winged child, swinging
on a swing like mine, a child
who every night went in to heaven.
You were an old man at first, with trailing beard,
then you were Blake's inventor god with compass,
but men were fallible, Father
bringing his things home from work in a cardboard box,
starting a business of his own, and failing
then starting again.

You were drink to my mother in the end
who measured freely her own death
from the green glass cup
she kept above the kitchen sink,
the vermouth left standing when she died,
cases and cases in the basement,
erect as missiles.
By then you had become
the purple spot inside my head when my eyes
close, the stars
with their nothing, beyond nothing.

Licking River

Cookies were served
and lemonade in paper cups.
They laid the bones out on the picnic table,
lamp at each end.
Each member of the boating party took her piece, and little
by little were parted
bones that had lain at the mouth
of the Licking,
a woman they said
judging from the pelvis.

Odd these bones on the rough
planked table, woods around
dark and stirring before the rain,
party chatter, flap
of the wooden screen door,
yellow cast of flame on wood and bone—
but I took the nail,
took it home.
Its shank warmed my palm,
the single letter I.

I Know I Dream of You

Old woman drinking death,
succumbing.

Everybody hates me, you say.
I love you.
Yes, you say, in admiration and pity,
you do love me.

You don't make it easy.
I scold you as my child.
You are shrinking:
everything's washed away except the sarcasm,
hardest substance in you.
More of you survives in me than in you.

Years ago, in some forgotten way station,
over lemonade I watched you closely.
You're memorizing me, you said.

Waking to Names of the Dead

Harold Arlen died today,
right on the heels of James Cagney and Wallis Simpson.
They follow you into the ground, an army
of ants at the close of a picnic,
your generation, Mother, your news.
They gassed the fields of France when you were ten:

ten, we knelt beneath our school desks.
Zero
was the center of the world:
to its right was everything, to its left
the ghost of everything.
You could take a big number
from a little number
but how could you have less than nothing left?

The shrapnel Uncle Ed carried home from the Argonne
rattled in his chest like coin:
it made him growl when he spoke,
the little box held tight against his throat.
Down at the end of the street lived a widow
who let me play with the rusted
toy trucks of her son killed in Bataan.

When Wallis Simpson became a widow,
you said of her marriage to the king, *A woman
should never force a man to choose.* And later,
The Japanese forced Truman to use the bomb.
Out of a job at the mill, you went back to the kitchen table
where weekday afternoons you fought
the old wars in books, waiting
for news of the world.

The Idea of Beauty

Back then the sun perched on the neighbors' roof
and milk stood pearled in sweat on the back porch.
You could hear its volume scrape against the cement step,
bottles removed and bottles received,
a sign of rising.

You slept past dawn beneath
the rafters of the parental roof, and the few stars,
the Dipper that still shone through,
had been there all night long for you, should you rise
and take out the window screen to study them.
You were safe then, but you didn't know it,

so you rose a little earlier than you needed to,
layering on the mascara, foundation, lipstick,
curling eyelashes, unrolling
the painful bristled rollers
you slept on fitfully.
It was like Broadway, your life every morning.

Breakfast was free and plentiful, the sun
firing red preserves on toast,
but you could barely eat half a slice,
and if you didn't eat, you got sick anyway.
What direction would you take to walk and who
would walk with you?

Terminal Moraine

The limestone walks of the city were covered with seashells
and the less common fossils of squid or trilobite.
The ocean had once been everywhere,
and the glacier thousands of years before
had dozed its slow path down,
pushing all the stones to a point over Cincinnati.
This is why we are hilly
and everything north is flat.
I used to think the land
flat as a page around Columbus

made my northern cousins simple.
We had the river, its periodic floodings,
and on sticky August afternoons
we lay on our backs on the stone porch
wishing the roadway under water
studded with luminous one-celled creatures
to which the spaniel panting on the tiles,
and you weeding, and ourselves
gazing through the bottoms of iced sodas,
could trace descent.

Crossing in the Dark

I meet you in the most unlikely places,
in the inky surface of the night water
moving against the hull of the ferry
like ancient skin, pooling at elbows and knuckles
broken but continuous,
translucent.

Last night's attic was crammed
with trivial and dangerous items. You knew
these were ideas, but I
thought they looked like furniture:
wardrobes with high mahogany wings,
darkened mirrors.

Moving from beneath you is
like swimming through salt water
these mornings in the dark.
Your weight presses out from my pelvis in frantic rings.
You watch the spasms of my sleep as you lie
evenly all up and down my bones.

You crease my cheek with the flat of your hand.
Your breaths
are my exhalations, my breaths are yours.
You are the body I cross as this ferry crosses the water
pushing against you to move forward,
marking you with my wide wake,
from slip to groaning slip.

The Body Opened

I. Theater Ruin

Rubbled seats, the fallen curtain and its counterweights,
velvet, brocade, brick dust,
the proscenium, its chipped masks smiling and frowning.

A temple to the dark, house of shadows.
The jazzman in his spangled suit eats his eternal hotdog
and watches one more movie through the glass,

mumbling old lovers to himself.
The shaggy woman in the marquee's shadow
warns as we pass.

And the projectionist who stashed
his television just outside the booth
is here too in some lost atom.

Mahogany and alabaster, colored glass,
the grassy smell of popcorn in the dark, the sweet
blue light swimming down from booth to screen

mixing and purling with the smoke, a transparent
marble path to memory:
through the gilded membrane of the dome
a sperm of daylight
swims the blank flesh of the screen.

Light is dissolving the body.
The body is opening to light.

II. Glastonbury Abbey

Read that the aging abbot was dragged
from behind the flaming altar, forced
to walk to the top of Glastonbury Tor,
an almost vertical ascent, and there
drawn and quartered, looking on his ruined abbey.

Drawn: *moved by traction, hauled, pulled, strained,*
    stretched, made thin by tension.

Quartered: *cut in quarters, divided in four,*
his bones scattered north, south, east, west,
to Wells, Bath, Ilchester, Bridgewater,
his head hung toothless from the gate.

Like Father, his still
flat body, its few peaks of bone beneath the sheets,
a broken arch, its half smile. And the town is built of these
    stones,
cruel as any child taking from the parent

exactly what it needs,
ex cathedra, *from the seat of learning.*
The church is the body of Christ, aisles
laid out in transepts like the cross,
four quarters.

III.

What does Body think as it lies there
dark, after the heart has cooled?

            ~   ~   ~

Body sings itself the old songs,
The Battle Hymn of the Republic in six verses or
I'm Forever Blowing Bubbles.
To keep awake, it hums parts
and sings parts,

*they fly so high
nearly reach the sky
then like my dreams
they fade and die.*

Body only wishes to receive the light
as it changes into all of its new guises:
a mushroom fruiting at the foot of a dead elm,
a star.

Remember the light, the exact
white of the forbidden sun. *Light.*
Long it would lie on my bones, and the birds
peeling the flesh away. But the light,
the light would be the last best lover.

Body can't remember why
it has been put away.
The dark seems familiar. Now
words of songs are breaking into one another

> *downyon dergreenval ley
> wherestream letsmeander
> wheretwi lightisfad ing
> Ipensi velyroam*

The words are falling like wet flakes.

IV.

Mother is a stone,
Father is the river:
in life it was the other way around.
Who knew which would make the moving ghost, which
the still?

Slowly they are learning to forget,
as one by one atoms
seek the company of other atoms:
carbon, hydrogen, oxygen.

They are more alive in this universe
than we who carry
the whole weight of memory:
who I am, who they were.

They are no more audience:
dead mother, dead father,
the gate we came in
lost now and overgrown.

We were always alone, the heart
beating in its solitary cave,
each breath after the first
a solemn duty, the body
always wise.

For them, a heaven if they want it,
or better still, long rest from memory.
A stone, weary now of talking, loving to be still.
The river, loose in syllables, continuous
now and flashing,
all movement.

Racing the Sun to New River Gorge

The Greenbriar river slips through my mirror, and the train
takes another turning.
    The river
appears again at the window
green as moldavite,
like moss but clear.

The window
the mirror and the river
are light gone and going: the mirror
stealing the river
each time,
then it's lost altogether to the hayfields, their neat

cylindrical bales laid like loaves on a pine board.
Two dark brown ponies peer down a ravine
as the train takes itself to darkness.
We're racing the sun to New River Gorge,
world's longest steel arch span,
but we'll never make it in what's left of this winter day.

Halfway to Cincinnati now, halfway home,
and this eve of my birthday likely more
than halfway through a life.
The Route Guide's notable stops
in boldface: Cincinnati, a white star in a black circle,
Indianapolis and Chicago, stars beyond.
Back there on the tracks Manassas, Culpeper

gone into the mirror
but I remain,
dredged in shadow like the rocks of the Gorge,
inky now, creased
and backlit as the light
pulls away.

When the Invisible Self Forgets

Outside the window of the Chinese restaurant
a man in dreadlocks talks
to someone no one else can see.
He seems to be pushing
that person into traffic.

Behind the steaming noodles
I remark to my reflection in the glass:
The body bags. . . .
(I have to move my lips to make her hear).
She says nothing, my invisible self.
Respecting our privacy, people look away.

> The downtown streets were flooded
> from a summer rain, currents
> so strong we were all
> afraid to cross.
> Then down they floated, the body bags,
> a green canvas Armada,
> every one feet first.

What happens when the invisible self forgets
to look both ways before crossing?
We might be walking up Broadway.
I say something,
she asks me to explain,
then a thump against a fender.
I carry her back to the hotel
and have our last conversation.

Hearts. White, Hanging

18—*The Aerialist*

Times Square Walking, 1969

42nd.

    LIVE GIRLS porno handbill hawker.
    Shuffling the peanut hidden beneath a cup
pockfaced hustler.

43rd
44th
At 45th a boy with scissors sells
    his girlfriend's hair as she lies
blissed out on the pavement.   The longing
to turn and run,
coddled-egg Ohio shyness I left
like a stocking on the sidewalk, but the voyeur
remains.

        Now

looking down from forty-seven floors and thirty-one more
    years
the globe and its continents flame orange over Broadway
THE STORM IS COMING.
Suntory Whiskey,
Coke's giant bottle, the emerging
and retiring straw:
        Above the yellow glide of taxis
Budweiser Clydesdales in two-story video, Nasdaq's
shifting numbers chased and chasing.
At Broadway and 7th, a giant bikini squats
sifts desert sand on her thigh.

It's all so hopeless, so eternal:
a cup of steaming noodles,
stepped ziggurat of smoked glass
we spy from our small window and
changing,
we draw our drapes.

        Victoria Hallerman—19

Date

Before the second date, I dreamt his right foot:
twice the size of mine, but still
perfectly formed, its big toe
an amiable paddle
and the ankle, sturdy
as a turning in white oak.
          My lover-soon-to-be-husband was giant, rare

as a Snow Leopard, and perhaps a little dangerous.
Of course he wasn't.   Dangerous.
          Although his mouth when it covered mine
in that soft eclipse of a kiss
could have smothered.
So could his whole virgin body
pressed against mine on a long-ago sofa,

but it didn't.
I have watched his right hand tear
 a door from its hinges.
I have beaten my fists into the dear
soft ground of his chest.
He has never struck me
though he wanted to.
How many have we been?

Late in the game,
eggs infrequent,
sperm count low,
we tried in a halfhearted way.
Pity the child to split
this twoness.
Years

          ~   ~   ~

and lovers later
spilled wax on the table between,
bones strewn, the gravy
pooled in shallow
salt licks on each plate,
palm on palm over flame
we keep right on.

Edge

I go for a glass of water
turn the tap to close it
and the porcelain wheel cracks in my hand
a cutting edge   blood
stains the bowl

     Life
is mostly edges:
knives and narrow planks,
iced stairs, highways, the wing
of the descending plane,
the unevenly balanced ladder,
a highwire.

                   Pear, apple, breast,
love is round.   Death is sharp, the incisor
straight and flat as a plank
or a well-hewn stone. It is·hard to remember we are round
not flat with an edge you can sail off straight into hell,
realm of the Kraken.   The sun and moon
are sharp discs
cutting through cloud and night sky.

Here's the edge of the conversation
where silence cuts and we are both left
alone and astonished.

The Road Home

Light slips over the asphalt at regular intervals,
road ghosts evading pressure of tire on pavement.
A three-dimensional hand waves from a billboard.
I cross the bridge.
Downriver the coffee cup empties two red drops
then collects them.
I could still have a child—

in this world that borders the turnpike,
its service areas named for cancer victims
or heroes.
I stop for gas at Walt Whitman.
Across the marshes the Empire State Building is sinking,
rocket on a collapsed pad.
Jersey is the lab of the world—
pipes with tongues of pale green flame,

domes and spirit-lamps.
Sometimes Newark smells like rubber bands.
The sports arena, concrete spider, hugs the flatland:
six white lights trail off from it like code.
A neon leaf greens itself
beneath the blackened grid of the Pulaski Skyway—
the egg in me moves down to the mouth of the world.

White Bleeding Hearts

Hearts. White hanging
in succession, parachutists wait
for the signal to jump.
There is that moment
before the chute opens

falling into earth—
not like a leap off the ten-foot board
or eleven stories to grim concrete
from a ledge—
here is plenty of time to fall.

Forget your stomach which dropped away already:
lie flat on air,
stretch your arms and limbs out and fall. Remember,
the cat turns herself even
in a few stories,

and prepares to land.
Trust the chute
copied from a floating seed-pod,
this heart accurate, seeking
Earth.

Appendix

Don't come home, I'm all right. What he didn't say:
It hurts to bend over and I haven't eaten in three days.
Walking hurt too, but he made it to the pharmacy.
Laxatives, they told him later, can kill.
So can working out with weights
to get things moving again.

He came within hours:
the angels of his morphine
talked among themselves.
Electrical storm: his own.
The scar, a new river from sternum to pelvis,
is what we have.

Keep it open
until it closes on its own,
the body saving itself as once
it wove a sac to contain
what no one understood
was rotting.

The Wound

Hands squeeze salt water into the crack
day after day, dressing it,
unreeling the gauze from its plush cavity.

The wound is a mouth, but nobody knows what it is saying.

It dies into a scar
and in the scar the body remembers

how deep was the division of flesh from flesh,
God parting the sea,
how tender the red slick waves,

all along the body working for closure,
leveling the fault,
pushing the riverbed closer and closer to surface.

Like water, the body heals itself,
each injustice raised to the surface,
examined, a splinter, and dismissed.

The wound keeps its own counsel:
it seals again the purse,
the wild balloon of the body.

2. The wound is a mask
lips painted *Cherries in the Snow*
over the truer mouth, the deeper invisible wound
that is open, incurable, festering, mortal.

~   ~   ~

In sleep the wound lies open,
the body open, and there are standing figures,
blood, a geyser of it, masks, and quickly moving hands.

Outside the tent of consciousness two angels
are having a conversation:
one is sure the sleeper will live, the other
less certain.

Summer haze, sizzling
crickets, butter lilies
folding open their tents of yellow silk—

the heart insists on beating in its tender red nest.
But now a slit has opened in the sky,
something has slipped through, and the wound
weeps secretly.

3. The navel:
gone
vanishing point at the end of a tunnel.
The wound erased it.
The scar

becomes now the central axis of the body
like a ruled line through a point—
the entry point into this world—
the knotted birthcord,
a feature of fleshly landscape and for that
beloved, a shrine.

                ~   ~   ~

4. The wound is a door.
Locked
but you can walk through it into sky,
into crenellated blue water.

You are on one side of the wound
and the sky is on the other side,
a sheet of blue cold-pressed paper.

Write on it with the invisible ink of your moving body.
The wound is a spirit-door.
You can't open it
you can't close it
but you can walk through it.

The Sea Is a Moving House

The sea is a moving house,
the roof-pitch changeable
the bed dark and unmade.
Enter at any point
nothing shatters, nothing
is torn,

the body is received whole.
The hull,
the honeymoon couple's trunk and readable papers
preserved in salt, dressing gown, checkbook,
teacups, the stairs to the first class cabin:
every discovery a loss,

every syllable
of air that found the surface from a filling lung,
what she said the last time
like the movement of the hand cutting the onion,
are lost along with pincer, shell, sea-glass,
sharp edges whetted now and safe.

Trailing violet warnings, jellyfish
pulse and surface,
a cormorant dips
then reappears, flashing
something silver and far off.

The Work of the Water

Life is lived between the hammer blows
of the carpenter next door:
the smoke alarm,
the burning toast, silence
at the other end of a ringing telephone,
a cement mixer grinding away at seaside,
the sun broken raw on the water.

Another day begins by the sea.
Perhaps these rocks will teach me how to wait
as they wait, patiently, for the water
to do its work of erosion.

He's gone away again to the city.
He keeps the lapping sound of the water
in the spiral of his inner ear
like the bubble in a carpenter's level,
like his own fluids of balance.

The carpenters are drilling on the house next door
that wasn't loved for its unplumbness
and had to be torn down
to its foundations.
Someone comes each night to check
the progress of the work,
but no one checks the work of the water:
a new crack opened in the rock,
a shard of cobalt glass deposited.

Swans in a Tidal Inlet

Those first two driven in by the Great Hurricane
fresh water birds who learned
to live in salt, to eat
the brine-soaked bread we toss.
    So many generations, one family in this cove:

each year four or five signets—gray
fluff in April, and by now
long of body, still gray but frosted white at the wingtips,
turning
                and gone white by winter.
How easily they blur to the eye

until they seem
a progression like the movement of water:
impossible to know where one wave ends.
We come here each year, loyal as any mating pair
but childless, and for each year

a new generation of swans.
Winter's seeming vacancy: the mounded
twig-nest insulated by snow
and her white patient body.
The clutch of eggs.   Heroism
is always an illusion—

you do what you do.
She sits in snow while he
protects her, moving in a wide arc
until, pricking its way, the fierce
first chick breaks open once again
this blue and rolling world.

Children's Art, Stormlight

Lightning
lights these painted blue green red and yellow sticks,
a kind of thunder nest, all hemp
and tempera.

Outside the door a dimesized spider
waits to ride the storm out in the cone of her web,
her most recent victim, a half-eaten living fly,
twitches, oblivious.

He'd asked about the thunder.
There is no storm. This is Intensive Care. All night long the
    nurse,
You in there Dean? Talk to me baby.
Death's random firings, his private storm.
Talk. Talk to me.

The painted friendship sticks hang parallel,
some forked, some straight,
dotted, striped or solid, the hemp knots clumsy
kids' work   far

from the spider's elegant snood.
I wake and touch his face. We talk.
The bundled sticks are stilled thunder, mythic bolts.
Our world is more or less one piece
this morning, storm
and spider gone.

Surfaces

In a dark theater masked lovers are kissing,
figures immobile at a walk light.

Gold-winged Gabriel kneels at table edge to whisper:
there's a bomb on the kitchen counter.
At open French windows the blue girl gazes on the pale green

mermaids of a North Dakota riverbank.
This woman's face is tight as a Brazil nut.
Give me truths, for I am weary of the surfaces.

Ultramarine

Here the sun comes from lower down:
it greets us at navel-height rising out of Cuba.
Other people's children drift
carelessly through the arches on the promenade, or play
mindless of the bride and groom vowing in the surf as the sun
declines.

Midnight-blooming jasmine is heavy on the air.
At dawn a woman two balconies up leans into the light:
I can still see the castle—it didn't wash away
she calls to her son.
Away, away, away, he sings back.

Snow? I hear from another balcony. *We're flying back into*
    SNOW?
A woman's voice. Desperate. *How much? When did it start?*
The winter ghost of Wallace Stevens swims
  the corridors of this hotel,
My north is leafless and lies in a wintry slime.

Last night's house on the edge
of a drained lake:
we filled the lake and the house lifted, groaning,
all the chandeliers swaying.

We stroll in continuous parade on the sand.
Our heroic legs and feet with their flying buttress toes
balance and throw balance and throw.
Small feet raised high in the air out of a pram,
round almost as the cushiony

~   ~   ~

tips of anemone,
will flatten someday soon and keep
their inaudible conversations with Earth.
We are pilgrims here to sun and sea, we have lost our watches.

—Key West, January, 1997

Late Season

Breath prints on the smudged kitchen window,
your nose flattened against the glass.
Eggplants set out foolishly late
blossom in the faded garden:

their sturdy purple blooms close
and fall.
Soup breathes from its iron pot,

a broth of onion and carrot and summer savory against the
    chill
you dissolve into.
Out of the soup of our daily lives
your belly and mouth and eyes would have come

my egg a tiny sun
his whip-tailed fish to split its core.
            All is safely gathered in:

Muskmelon, corn, blueberries,
said the man at the farm stand,
everything you've got is the last of something.
Tonight's a full moon. Harvest moon?

        Shine on, shine on,
sings Daddy from underground.
You could sing too, if you had breath.   Once or twice

we invited you to our table,
but you never came.
Month's end, you'll be any one of the hands
reaching into the Halloween bowl.
        ~   ~   ~

Body asks itself what's next?
Going down, this unsplit sun,
this fish, restless turning alongside.

How It Is

The house on the hill, Tudor, cream and brown, his dream: I live inside. The one with the whale weather vane that turns, screaming every January and threatens to leave the roof-peak; with a stripling maple in the side yard, brought down by *Isabelle* on her way west. Inside, a balcony for looking down on the ghosts passing daily through our living room, in and out, above, below, and through the twenty-four-electric-candle chandelier: the house we shared with too many people until we just wanted to be alone. It's our story, every closet full of failures or half-schemes: the footlight gels from the theater; chef tunics with nineteen-year-old beet stains; pans, chemicals, filters, the contents of a defunct darkroom; boxes from "The Great Talking Mannequin Concern." Once I wanted a couple of rooms in the city, but I never said so; then he announced, "I've found a house," and I went right along. It was a real house, finer than the one I grew up in, and looking on the harbor. Foggy mornings, I wake to boat horns. The garden holds half my life measured off in Sundays spent planting feverfew, Great Solomon's Seal, bleeding heart. I'm not young anymore, but the garden doesn't seem to notice, sending mint and trillium through the crust each spring. The one-story walk-up I always thought I'd have is a particular kind of memory; that's how it is with marriages that last. What you never did is like that sealed stone room under the porch. Who knows what's in there?

Aerialist

Her life is the wire—she can never come down.
Sometimes she stops and sits on it to eat,
even sleeps there, her whole body stretched
as the wire is stretched. In sleep
she keeps her balance,
feet curled like a monkey's,
the habit of grasping:

she has never fallen.
She never will, not entirely.
Once in a while a slip
causes her to hang for a moment by her hands.
It isn't the danger of falling that slices through her dreams
but the wire itself, drawing
a line through her body,
leaving a mark on the soles of her feet,

her buttocks, her back.
If she were to cut the wire (she dreams of this)
the sky would break like a mirror into the sea
and nothing would be whole again.
Virgin of the Apocalypse standing on a crescent moon,
she is keeping
Heaven and Earth apart.

Victoria Hallerman—39

The Woman in the Magic Show

A House

In each room a spiral stair. She's
descending like the famous nude.
Frames of a film all exactly the same
nothing like it except

maybe Warhol's *Empire:*
eight unblinking hours of the same building,
her body as it ages, as lights
dim in some cells,
stay on a while in others.

Even as the outside changes, as hair
forgets its reddish yellow-brown
and nails split,
genes still send their insistent
message   *me*
over and over.

In her saliva on the back of a stamp
more than in the message it delivers,
and on her comb, flecks of scalp.   Stray hairs
coil near the bed where every night for years
she's filed in perfect code the snagged
edges of herself.

Sculpture by George Segal

They've been standing at the light
so long they've turned to salt.
Maybe they're confused because
it says WALK, DON'T WALK.
The man in the foreground has forgotten
where he is, wide stance,
hands in pockets.
He'd be meditating if he weren't
ash-white and immobile.
They might be enchanted,
folks who've stepped into a fairy ring—
a hundred years won't age them a minute.
They'll wake up, the light will change
and they'll have the whole planet
to themselves.

We grew up playing bomb shelter

and it didn't happen:
that is what we love about the past.

Against the blackened chimney stacks of Toledo

Mother and Don as children are looking at something
beyond the edge
Late afternoon, 1915.

Her last picture:
She drifts among the Queen Anne's lace
for all her bulk, weightless as a flower.

I have no pictures of myself, no children
and history?
who will remember—

I want to bury a few things in the garden
like the map floating in space—
man, woman, the coordinates of Earth.

Victoria Hallerman—45

Seeking Ground

The day lightning split that oak
from branchtip to root, two hundred feet of tree,
Gramp bit through his pipe as the knife of light
blazed to a glowing orange ball.

Celestial
strayed from the courts of heaven,
it bounced off the tarmac and vanished
like the risen Jesus.

It was Sunday, after all.
The lamb burned on in the oven.
Great Aunt Marie, who hadn't walked in fifteen years,
dropped her cane and ran three times around the kitchen table.

Fire dwells in earth, waits
for the sky-twin;
a hand touches a hand in a mirror.

Tiny fires of synapse in my hand
signal fires, campfires;
the brain tells the hand
                    Don't touch that.

Seeking ground, the negative
yearns for the positive in every shivering cell:
in ball or sheet or fork, the light
longs for its home in darkness.

At the Boat Basin

I shed several more selves, the teacher
fretted away last night, the homeowner,
back turned on the dirty, half-painted house.

Selves come and selves go, like the marsh birds here—
egret, heron—who arrive and depart from this quiet
    confluence
of river and sea with little effort, or so it seems.

Only the songbirds, permanent residents,
give the impression of labor.
Once at twilight as I walked, a small tree

shook with a voice
so operatic it filled the basin.
Deep in its branches a redwing blackbird

sang us all the way to darkness.

Doll in a Suitcase
—for Charlotte DeRuiter Wirthlin, 1883-1973

Childless
and widowed by the time you came unstrung,
she packed you in a suitcase
as the dead are sometimes packed in jars—
eyes, hair, teeth, fingers—you were
chambered as any princess made ready for a journey
up some muddy river dark
as home.

In the year of her death we found you
your thigh holes empty
your porcelain head resting on a nest of wooden limbs,
 a fall of her mother's hair
brittle those seventy-odd years, still red
and winking from the satin pocket on the suitcase lid.

The dollman warned as he re-strung you,
These old babies are hard to live with. Sure enough,
you moved inside me: your plump
archaic smile with its seed-pearl teeth,
hard, perfect blush, stilled eye.
The red hair witching you,
I tried to wake. You were never a plaything:

you sat those days of her childhood
high up on her wardrobe
as you've sat these twenty-six years since,
a patient guest in my livingroom,
never aging, in need of a curl and a wash,
lips parted on a wild
red verge.

Hudson River Frozen Across at Rhinecliff

This wedding cake:
here and there waves crested and froze
as the spatula shaped them, bending
away at each stroke from the surface.
Thin drag of a serrated blade through icing,
the tanker pauses from its work of cutting a channel.
Just now

it is hard to believe in the movement of water
but at Poughkeepsie the channel widens, and the Hudson
seems more like its old reliable self, getting up
sluggish from a long nap.
Under the dulled glow of a winter sun,
all the way down to New York, it's opening

slowly to tugs, tankers and barges,
to the business of the world and to the salt
greeting of the sea.
Traffic is making the river ready,
breaking it into foot-thick slabs of ice
you could just lie down and go to sleep on,
drifting south.

Each town has its boatyard
and each boatyard,
like the river itself, is sleeping,
boats snug in their harsh blue tarps.
The only visible life is a tavern here or there,
with its neon shamrock.
But it is just as well we can't stop,

for there is a loneliness in each daily life
that we behind the glass of a moving train
are free to imagine:
the river's fish beneath the ice,

~   ~   ~

Victoria Hallerman—49

survivors, kiss
the underside for its thin
layer of air.

Dervish

The wind is scratching and howling
the wind is banging the unlatched door   rubbing
its haunches against the house

a phrase causes the body to twitch and sway
a single syllable rolling
and circling in the mouth

the ecstatic syllable   the first word
that catches in the throat
the wind is holding the house like a drum

the wind is beating on the taut
skin of the house
of the heart   it kindles

the song burns first in the heart and the throat
dry and insistent
it reaches the floor of the mouth
and explodes

let it out
let it out to touch the wind
it will blaze there
or burn the house down

You as a Gambling Table

To die is what you said you wanted,
leaving the green glass measuring cup you kept above the sink,
a ration of cheap vermouth freely poured.

I missed you a long while,
our Friday morning calls
—not the visits home, you passed out on the sofa—
just the calls, book talk, small talk.

Free.   It was
my world and you had no more opinions.
I would build my own life, different from yours.
give up on children, stay married,
write and teach.

Not so fast.
Here you are risen in your green sleep,
and you are not my life, but it seems
you are the place it happened,
the felted green table my life
plays itself out on.

In a notebook I kept twenty-one years ago,
your voice
like a drop of absinthe.

Every decision I make: the well-considered
tight shot, the hasty slam
comes back somehow to one of your pockets:
what you expected,
what you failed to expect.

Husk

I is heavy, a brocade coat
I'm sewn into, a shroud,
a hymen, a foreskin, a chrysalis,
husk of a locust not shed.
After I die   I will stand

alone, absurdly capital
at certain intersections of my life's text,
directing traffic.
It is possible in dreams to leave
amnesiac, to enter some new life:

what are these cracks on the kitchen wall
so familiar, the blue-rimmed cup of another life?
mine, not mine.
Me is the proud *I* rounded, split
the object, humble

touched, never touching.
It listens, never speaks.
Ice,
fire quiver in me—
I describe them.

Inert as rock, slippery, *me*
can't hold a verb,
but the juice at the bottom of the pickle jar
and the vertigo of death
belong to me.

Woman, I put you on each day,
sew you up, even to the eyelids.

Ash Grove

Seeds of words under the tongue:

take these words, first of a morning
holding, let them
dissolve, one body
into another.
What words
once were, syllables

round or rough
reached for with your tongue
as eye reached for light
and shapes that turned in the space above the crib.
Syllables were globes or cones or
isolated jigsaw pieces with chewed corners.

Then the lyrics of the song
downyondergreenvall
eyas
streamletsmeander
became a valley and small streams and that word
meander!   You grew

into the text.
Below, still
                  you can listen
for the underground river, ecstatic
syllable that shifts
in its course
and outruns the meaning.

The Woman in the Magic Show

The lily opens,
its brown velvet glove tips erect,
its speckled yellow silk
folded under, opening all the way
like a woman whose eyes are closed in fantasy.
And even if it is a memory she opens to,
how delicious the splitting
of the selves, right and left,

as in the magic show, she is whole
and sawed in half at once,
like the newly-dead whose souls
hover regarding themselves,
then dissolve into atoms.
Supposing

you are the woman in the magic show
indivisible even by the saw,
you bow low as the audience
marvels, then you are split
lengthwise this time,
just like a tree split by lightning:
and each half has one eye, one hand, one ventricle,
one lung, one hemisphere of brain, one breast,
no navel, no clitoris, no tongue.

You Pass

He said, "I think you take the world the dead
have left you,
you change it in a small way, and you pass it on."

    I slept,
got up and unplugged all the phones,
read snippets of three books and a magazine,
drank half a cup of Oolong,
walked the dog

        noticed the way the sea
beyond the window blurs in the cross
-hatches of the screen, and how
those hatches blur as the cormorant dives.
The world at my touch still hadn't changed

one syllable, unless
you count the fact that we went out to the road,
the dog and I, and he
grazed a bit—
come to think of it, he shat—and so
left something of himself behind.
        What have I left?

If a dog can pass a dill seed
through his gut to sprout and flower, what about
my words waiting
for the accident of eyes to touch them?
I try
first just to hold on

    ~   ~   ~

to the channels of last night's mackerel sky,
the lamb with spinach and ravioli,
bright points in the darkening eyes of a friend I'll never see.
Some things will fall away, much will pass
stubborn as tomato seed through the heat
of memory to who knows
what second life.

Page

Blank but already
           the light plays on its surface
                          mirror-chip
      waves,

quicker even than the leaping
of oil in a hot skillet:
           sauté.
There is this movement at the surface of language

the unwritten word in the page meets the word
on the tongue, in the eye.

On this day
           when water can barely hold off sky,
there are paths in the sea where the wind
has walked it smooth.

This blank page
      is all that keeps me

from the slice of forgetfulness my body
longs to have this morning on the sofa
before the fire built to take the damp out of this house.

Where has the wind walked?   Its paths
are vanishing.   Water and sky
are the same flat tone of chalk, whole

as desert to a new rider.
Uncut, the cake of the page.   Hope
of this life.

Hurry On

Crazy first commuters:
every ferry has them, running
who knows to what missed appointment,
rendezvous, drug deal,
each possessed of a hurry-demon,
a fire at every back.

Then the rest of us: the shoeshine hobbles off with his
    kit,
brisk-walking the broker with briefcase, the woman pushing a
    stroller.
Never still until
finally at night another kind of movement
takes each sleeper: rapid eye, involuntary
twitch, synapse.   Somewhere

running continuous to rock
breakers of the night shore,
the gray resolute surf rolling just behind,
and the horizon seeming so still
itself turning and turning to show or to hide
sun or moon.

Hurry on, Earth,
for what is truly still
here is dead:
the infant like a stone
rolls into the morgue,
a possum, bone and fur

~   ~   ~

half-buried in the lettuce patch.
Silence and the last step,
something mineral spins past,
                an angel
goes unobserved to work in the garden.
Meanwhile

this body with its fingers and toes,
five and five   five and five
and its breath continuous, the heart
stoical as any commuter, one beat, one step at a time

I am not alone
I am not alone.

Night Market

Be still voices.
All the chirping voices
contending for light and air,

bartering memories or clever endings to stories
wish endings of true stories
as the ice cream vendor sells his lies in sweet white cups.

Here is the rain of morning come to quiet all,
the plain voice of the rain like a prophet.
Day is walking and all the close bodies of the night market

scatter.
Day is another kind of dream, the one
we have in common.

Straight

Each day's
the straightest
and slenderest of highways
taut from point to point
like a line drawn with a ruler into space.   There is
nothing in nature so unforgiving

not the horizon with its foolish curve   lip
of Earth against the dark   not
the most perfect of pines which stretching
for light has still
some sway in its trunk.   Here
is a narrow path: no

stepping off
though it's so overgrown
dense with ropy and dark-faced
shapes   you might as well
walk blindfold   trusting
only your ear and your sure foot.

Oh you will fall
no matter how far you've come
in a heartbeat over the edge
and yet a few
will call after you
leaning forward
that moment into the dark.

Out of the Bottle-Glass Tower

Out of the bottle-glass tower you came
a goddess rolled in foil

Out of the house made from heads of dolls
you came with your flesh/not flesh

Out of the cave one man carved in desert rock
you came as wind

Out of the house made of musical instruments
broad and low as a piano, you came singing

Where the fairy child swings on a sunset swing
there you lived in your pennanted castle

You dwelt with Emily in *a fairer house than prose*

With the child who built her house of rice and beans and
    oranges
hoping to have enough to eat, you lingered

and in the dome of Union Terminal
you rested in the bodies of the workmen

From the purified copper steeple of the burning church
you came and they sang you into air

Burning in every stick of incense you filled the closet-temple
you smudged the lips and eyelids of the goddess

Out of a single pumping heart you run
as a river runs trusting its course

the houses and taverns settled on your banks dream
without turning

Victoria Hallerman—63

A Last Cloud

1.

It folds its creamy mouth around the sun
and someone in a laboratory garden
names a rose: *Iceberg* or *Eclipse*. Roses
are never named for deadlines, though there are
dark roses, so almost black the light
sinks in like matter approaching a dead star
or ship's planking on the lip of a maelstrom.
They would eat the sun if it came close enough,
these roses, their petals hard as tar.
No one named a rose for Hiroshima
which produced its own peculiar bloom
reminding some flyers of Creation,
the Big Bang, that first quarter-second,
when all the helium for balloons was new.

2.

When all the helium for balloons was new
the Cosmos was a kettle at peak boil
and all the bubbles spoiling to get out.
The gassy islands drifted loosely touching,
like Adam and his god.
They're drifting still: some galaxies
would take longer for us to reach
than the universe is old.
But we know from their billion-year-old light
they share flat space and once
chafed with us in a kettle so intense
the vapor may have formed a single bubble,
the universe, where on a speck some drunk
plows the wrong way through the Holland Tunnel.

3.

He plows the wrong way through the Holland Tunnel
and gets halfway before the backs of his
opponent's eyes turn over like two eggs
at a rolling boil, that second before impact
and nowhere to go but up.
Beyond the glass and flames, beyond the tile
zipper of the tunnel, mindful of the knot below,
the second driver, weightless, sheds his pain.
In Metuchen his wife warms dinner.
The drunk'll do some time, they're throwing the book
at him, manslaughter, reckless endangerment—
but he was only trying to die;
blinded, he will always dream in color.

4.

Blinded, he will always dream in color
the way the dead dream of the living:
they dream of skin that bruises, the kitchen
on a January night and coffee
in a chipped green cup, the table set for them.
Tired of smiling in their photographs,
they hear their names and no one hears them answer.
They linger in the brilliant wards, or in
a basement stairwell where the beating stopped.
This is frozen statues, that game we played—
you dance until the caller says to freeze.
if we could see the ultraviolet rays
or just the infrared, we could see them,
the unhappy dead, foresting the earth.

Burning Mulberry

Rekindle the three blackened ends,
last night's fire: there's warmth
turn it over, see the red belly of fire in the wood still.

Fire seeks fire:
lay one ember against the next.
Smoke rises, the sun

fires undersides of cloud,
touches Earth.
The new mother rises from her bed,

blood in her fingertips, and touches the child.
Eyes ignite,
banked down in the ashes of evening.

Hand against heart makes flame:
leave spaces for the fire to breathe,
red stamen of the Chrysanthemum
red at its heart.

On the Ferry, Reading Lives of the Astronomers

I measured the skies, now I measure the shadows
Skybound was the mind, the body now rests in earth.

—Johannes Kepler

As the doors to the ferryboat open,
the waiting push forward towards home.
All who are standing now will ride across the harbor.
Everyone else is bedded down for the night—
they lie on the benches like smooth-worn stones
just out of reach of water.
We who pass through the doors are the transients;
we keep our homes by leaving them each morning,

then, at night, we're like guards
closing down the hall of antiquities,
and all the torsos and reclining
tomb figures seem about to speak.
From the back deck Manhattan
forms an earthly constellation
and it is comforting to imagine
each illuminated small square a life
safe, accounted for.

Somewhere out there the stars themselves
are far from perfect
in their expanding and contracting universe,
the lung of God.
Broke and far from home,
Kepler died pointing to the stars
then to his head, then
back again.

~   ~   ~

Victoria Hallerman—67

The planets
went right on spinning in their dark
imperfect orbits
elliptical, as he had known,
faster
nearing the sun.

I find my words in a drawer

someone else's,
the woman ten
or twenty years ago
who remembers
the woman thirty years ago.
So do I.

Who am I?
Asked at the beginning:
a fortuneteller's query.
Asked in the middle:
a calling out to figures on ice floes
still recognizable, receding.
Asked at the end:
Who was I?

Moab. July, 1989

The desert has its furniture,
the Book Cliffs, Chimney Rocks,
mesas, Doll House Buttes—
we furnish it with the things we know.
And God is here too, the builder,
through whose canyons like supplicants
we crawl in our '71 Torino.
Will it overheat and leave us to the sun's bald gaze?

In the Professor's Canyon the hippies have their mailboxes
row on row, like tiny cave-dwellings on a post.
And all the roseate cliffs are laughing.
The Anaszazi left their drawings in the blue-black desert
   varnished rock:
bears and warriors with spiral shields,
lines of dancing figures holding hands,
advancing and receding through time,
and Bob and MaryAnne were here in '75.

To the rocks it's all graffiti
like the poems of Homer mixed in with occasional verse.
The yellow and black highway sign across the road with
   pointing arrow
reads INDIAN WRITINGS.
We look past it to the rock walls on the other side of the river.
Through the narrow glass tubes of the binoculars
at the mouth of a cave we have discovered,
a white patch of light becomes the blaze
on the face of a single dark brown horse.

Still, as in a trance, no bridle or saddle,
yet clean and shining.

~   ~   ~

We think the stallion sees our movements—he backs
into the cave and leaves us,
our vision trained on nothing for what seems
like ten whole minutes.
He re-emerges, crops some grass outside the cave.
So perfect. So perfectly alive.

Egret

Which of the angels is bringing me this morning's light?
Bright as the wings of annunciation,
the waking mind receives it, as Mary
in a fourteenth-century room, her books
and teakettle arranged carefully about her
receives her kneeling angel, and the tiny
seed of Christ swims in a mote of light through the open
    window

bearing its infinitesimal cross.
So each day brings the holy ghost of reason
back to us just when we had despaired of it,

and gives us one another's company,
animals who need to move and breathe and eat.
Tall and white as a communion candle, the egret
is a bird made of light, thin enough
to slip through the vanishing point of horizon, her neck

the spout of an amphora, legs spindles,
wings long-fingered hands, full when she spreads them
and hangs her white line of a body between them.

The stronger the light becomes the harder
it is to remember the exact temperature of the dream,
toes numb, heart almost still.
The room just left was carved out of ice
and even though the candle there burns
blue and cold,
the egret leans out from the rock into the light of this
    ordinary morning.

About the Author

Victoria Hallerman is a poet and educational literacy consultant who lives and works in New York City. Her poems have been published in a wide variety of magazines and anthologies including *Poetry, The Nation, Runes, Southern Poetry Review, Pivot, Global City Review, Indiana Review,* and *The L.A. Review,* among others. She has been a winner of "Discovery"/*The Nation,* The Red Hen Press/*L.A. Review* Prize, and *The Pushcart Prize.* Her full-book manuscript, *The Aerialist,* was the first runner-up last year for Sarabande's Kathryn A. Morton Prize and the winner of the Bright Hill Press Poetry Book Competition 2003. She has published two chapbooks and serves as an editor of *Heliotrope, a Journal of Poetry.*

Victoria is also currently at work on a memoir, *Surviving the Cure,* a chronicle of the effect prostate cancer and its treatment has had on her marriage.

About the Book

The type and layout of *The Aerialist* were designed by Bertha Rogers, as was the cover. The typeface for the text and cover is Adobe InDesign CS Garamond. The book was printed on 60-lb. offset, acid-free, recyled paper in the United States of America. This first edition is limited to copies in paper wrappers.

Other Bright Hill Press Books

Poetry and Fiction Collections

Gobbo, A Solitaire's Opera, David Capella (forthcoming) $8
First Place, 2004 Poetry Chapbook Award
Bright Hill Press At Hand Poetry Chapbook Series

Degrees of Freedom, Nicholas Johnson (forthcoming) $8
Second Place, 2004 Poetry Chapbook Award
Bright Hill Press At Hand Poetry Chapbook Series

Autobiography of My Hand, Kurt Olsson (forthcoming) $8
Third Place, 2004 Poetry Chapbook Award
Bright Hill Press At Hand Poetry Chapbook Series

In Late Fields, Steven Ostrowski (forthcoming) $8
Fourth Place, 2004 Poetry Chapbook Award
Bright Hill Press At Hand Poetry Chapbook Series

Instinct, Joanna Straughn (forthcoming) $8
Fifth Place, 2004 Poetry Chapbook Award
Bright Hill Press At Hand Poetry Chapbook Series

Walking Back the Cat, Lynn Pattison (forthcoming) $8
Third Place, 2003 Poetry Chapbook Award
Bright Hill Press At Hand Poetry Chapbook Series

The Spirit of the Walrus, ElisaVietta Ritchie (forthcoming) $6
Fourth Place, 2003 Poetry Chapbook Award
Bright Hill Press At Hand Poetry Chapbook Series

LightsOut, Tom Lavazzi $6
Second Place, 2003 Poetry Chapbook Award
Bright Hill Press At Hand Poetry Chapbook Series

Flares and Fathoms, Margot Farrington $12
Bright Hill Press Poetry Series

Strange Gravity, Lisa Rhoades, $12
2002 Poetry Book Award - Chosen by Elaine Terranova
Bright Hill Press Poetry Book Award Series

Possum, Shelby Stephenson $6
2002 Poetry Chapbook Award
Bright Hill Press At Hand Poetry Chapbook Series

First Probe to Antarctica, Barry Ballard $6
2001 Poetry Chapbook Award
Bright Hill Press At Hand Poetry Chapbook Series

The Singer's Temple, Barbara Hurd $12
2001 Poetry Book Award - Chosen by Richard Frost
Bright Hill Press Poetry Book Award Series

Inspiration Point, Matthew J. Spireng $6
2000 Poetry Chapbook Award
Bright Hill Press At Hand Poetry Chapbook Series

Other Bright Hill Press Books (cont.)

Heart, with Piano Wire, Richard Deutch $12
2000 Poetry Book Award - Chosen by Maurice Kenny
Bright Hill Press Poetry Book Award Series

Every Infant's Blood: New & Selected Poems, Graham Duncan $14.95
Bright Hill Press Poetry Series

What Falls Away, Steve Lautermilch $6
1999 Poetry Chapbook Award
Bright Hill Press At Hand Poetry Chapbook Series

My Father & Miro & Other Poems, Claudia M. Reder $12
1999 Poetry Book Award - Chosen by Colette Inez
Bright Hill Press Poetry Book Award Series

Boxes, Lisa Harris $6
1998 Fiction Chapbook Award
Bright Hill Press At Hand Chapbook Series

Traveling Through Glass, Beth Copeland Vargo $12
1998 Poetry Book Award - Chosen by Karen Swenson
Bright Hill Press Poetry Book Award Series

Whatever Was Ripe, William Jolliff $6
1997 Poetry Chapbook Award
Bright Hill Press At Hand Poetry Chapbook Series

To Fit Your Heart into the Body, Judith Neeld $12
1997 Poetry Book Award - Chosen by Richard Foerster
Bright Hill Press Poetry Book Award Series

Low Country Stories, Lisa Harris $6
1996 Fiction Chapbook Award
Bright Hill Press Chapbook Award Series

Blue Wolves, Regina O'Melveny $12
1996 Poetry Book Award - Chosen by Michael Waters
Bright Hill Press Poetry Book Award Series

The Man Who Went Out for Cigarettes, Adrian Blevins,
1995 Poetry Chapbook Award
Bright Hill Press Chapbook Award Series

My Own Hundred Doors, Pam Bernard
1995 Poetry Book Award - Chosen by Carol Frost
Bright Hill Press Poetry Book Award Series

Anthologies & Others

Bright Hill Book Arts 2005 (forthcoming) $14
Edited by Bertha Rogers
Bright Hill Exhibition Series

Fantastic! The Word Thursdays
Workshops for Kids 2004-05 Anthology (forthcoming) $12
Edited by Bertha Rogers - BH Books by and for Kids

Victoria Hallerman—75

Anthologies & Others (cont.)

Bright Hill Book Arts 2005 (forthcoming) $14
Edited by Bertha Rogers with Edward Hutchins
Bright Hill Exhibition Series

Bright Hill Book Arts 2004 $12
Edited by Bertha Rogers
Bright Hill Exhibition Series

Bright Hill Book Arts 2003 $10
Edited by Bertha Rogers
Bright Hill Exhibition Series

On the Watershed: The Natural World
of New York's Catskill Mountain Region $14.95
Poetry & Prose by Catskill Student Writers, Illustrated
Edited by Bertha Rogers

The Second Word Thursdays Anthology $19.95
Poetry, Fiction, & Nonfiction by Word Thursdays Authors
Edited by Bertha Rogers

The WT Summer & Winter Workshops for Kids
1998 Anthology $10
BH Books by and for Kids - Edited by Bertha Rogers

Iroquois Voices, Iroquois Visions $12
Edited by Bertha Rogers - Contributing Editors
Robert Bensen, Maurice Kenny, Tom Huff

Out of the Catskills & Just Beyond $24.95
Literary & Visual Works by Catskill Writers & Artists,
with a Special Section by Catskill High-School
Writers & Artists
Edited by Bertha Rogers

The Word Thursdays Anthology
Edited by Bertha Rogers

Speaking the Words Anthology
Edited by Bertha rogers

Ordering Bright Hill Press Books

BOOKSTORES: Bright Hill Press books are distributed to the trade by Small Press Distribution, 1814 San Pablo Ave., Berkeley, CA 94702-1624; Baker & Taylor, 44 Kirby Ave., POB 734, Somerville, NJ 08876-0734; and North Country Books (regional titles), 311 Turner St., POB 217, Utica, NY 13501-1727. Our books may also be found at BarnesandNoble.com and Amazon.com.

INDIVIDUALS: If your local bookstores do not stock Bright Hill Press books, please ask them to special order, or write to us at Bright Hill Press, POB 193, Treadwell, NY 13846-0193 or to our e-mail address: wordthur@stny.rr.com, or by telephone at 607-829-5055. Further information may be found on our web site: www.brighthillpress.org.

Order Form (may be duplicated)

(Note: Shipping and handling is $2.50 for the first book, and $1.00 for each additional book)

Title_____ Quantity_____Price_____

Title _____ Quantity_____Price_____

Shipping & Handling_____

SubTotal_____

Sales Tax_____

(New York State Residents, and where Applicable. Note: We cannot process orders without payment of applicable sales tax.)

Note: Orders of 3 or more, subtract 20% from total before sales tax.

Member discount (Subtract 10% from total before sales tax)_____

Ship to_____

Address_____

City_____State_____Zip Code_____

CHECK OR MONEY ORDER: AMT. ENCL. $_____

(total includes price of book(s), plus shipping & applicable taxes)

MasterCard_____VISA____

Card Account Number_____

Card Expiration Date_____

Customer Signature_____

Customer Tele. #_____E-mail_____

Card-issuing Bank Name_____